Contents

Introduction 5
What Is Gastroparesis? 7
    What causes gastroparesis? 8
    Who's at risk for developing gastroparesis? 9
    What are the symptoms of gastroparesis? 10
Gastroparesis Diagnosis 12
How is gastroparesis treated? 14
    Medication 14
    Surgery 15
    Diet changes 16
Experimental treatment options 17
    Botulinum toxin type A 17
    Vagal nerve stimulation 18
What are the complications of gastroparesis? 18
    Outlook 20
Surgery for gastroparesis 20
    Are there any other treatments for gastroparesis? 21
    Should I change my diet if I have gastroparesis? 22
    Foods to eat if you have gastroparesis 23
Gastroparesis recovery diet 25

Diet tips 26

Gastroparesis Recovery Diet Recipes 27

Best Diet for Gastroparesis 28

The Three-Phased Diet Approach 29

Essential Long-Term Diet Tips 31

Sample Gastroparesis Diet Plan 33

Sample 3-Day Diet Plan.. 34

Gastroparesis and the Low FODMAP Diet 36

GLUTEN FREE RECIPES 38

Gluten free Appetizers... 38

Lion's Den Lobster Fritters (Gluten Free)........................ 38

Gluten-Free Nuts and Seeds Clusters 40

Keto Sausage Balls.. 42

Lasagna-Stuffed Mushrooms 44

Fava Bean Breakfast Spread... 46

Scalloped Potatoes for the BBQ 47

Crab Stuffed Mushrooms.. 48

Bacon and Date Appetizer 50

Buffalo Cauliflower... 51

Low-Carb Almond Garlic Crackers 52

GLUTEN FREE BREAKFAST AND BRUNCH RECIPES 54

Momma's Potatoes... 54

Feta Eggs 55

Bacon Breakfast Casserole (Gluten Free) 56

Berry Good Smoothie II 59

Sweet Potato and Banana Pancakes 60

Mango Coconut Chia Pudding 61

Country style fried Potatoes 63

Delicious Gluten Free Pancakes 64

Sarah's Apple Sauce 65

Sauteed Apples 66

Greek Scrambled Eggs 67

GLUTEN FREE MAIN DISHES 68

Rump Roast Au Jus 68

Grilled Sea Bass 69

Chick Pea Curry 70

Fish Fillets Italiano 71

Rosemary Braised Lamb Shanks 72

Rosemary Braised Lamb Shanks 74

Texas Ranch Chicken 75

Brown Rice, Broccoli, Cheese and Walnut Surprise 77

Indian Style Sheekh Kabab 79

Paleo Pecan-Maple Salmon 81

GLUTEN FREE SIDE DISH 83

Sugar Snap Peas with Mint 83

Herbed Mushrooms with White Wine.............................. 84

Fried Plantains.. 85

Brandied Candied Sweet Potatoes 86

Corned Beef Potato Pancakes 87

Mediterranean Vegetable Cakes...................................... 89

Carrot Cake Quinoa 93

Easy Quinoa Mac And Cheese.. 94

Cathy's Gluten-Free Oatmeal Waffles 96

GLUTEN FREE DESSERTS 98

Buckeyes I 98

Chocolate Chip cookies.. 99

Chocolate Peanut Butter Bars 101

Amazing Gluten-Free Layer Bars 103

Perfect Flourless Orange Cake 105

Lemon Souffle 107

Irish Potato Candy 109

Angel Food Candy.. 110

Conclusion.. 113

Introduction

If you find yourself feeling extremely full after eating only a small amount of food, or feeling nauseated and throwing up after eating, don't brush it off as indigestion or lack of appetite. These could be warning signs of a digestive condition called gastroparesis. Gastroparesis (abbreviated as GP) represents a clinical syndrome characterized by sluggish emptying of solid food (and more rarely, liquid nutrients) from the stomach, which causes persistent digestive symptoms especially nausea and primarily affects young to middle-aged women, but is also known to affect younger children and males. Diagnosis is made based upon a radiographic gastric emptying test. Diabetics and those acquiring gastroparesis for unknown (or, idiopathic) causes represent the two largest groups of gastroparetic patients; however, numerous etiologies (both rare and common) can lead to a gastroparesis syndrome.While difficult to treat, a special gastroparesis diet can help to control symptoms. When you have gastroparesis, the amount of fats and fiber that you eat can greatly affect how intense your symptoms are.

The gastroparesis diet is always the first step to treating this condition after diagnosis. The easy-to-digest foods it promotes put less stress on your gastrointestinal system, reducing a range of uncomfortable symptoms such as nausea, vomiting, acid reflux, bloating, and abdominal pain.

Furthermore, the focus on nutrient density helps your body weather bouts of appetite loss that often arise during flare-ups. Without a consistent focus on good nutrition, these episodes could lead to malnutrition and weight loss.

Following a gastroparesis diet may also help you avoid medications and other treatments for the condition that may be associated with side effects.

What Is Gastroparesis?

Gastroparesis is a disorder in which the stomach empties extremely slowly — a meal that can be digested in about four hours in a healthy person may take days to empty out of the stomach of someone with gastroparesis, says Francisco J. Marrero, MD, a gastroenterologist with the Digestive Disease Institute at the Cleveland Clinic in Ohio. Gastroparesis results when the vagus nerve, which contracts the stomach to squeeze food further down the digestive tract, becomes damaged in some way.

Gastroparesis is an extremely rare condition, affecting only about 10 out of every 100,000 people, according to Dr. Marrero. The condition can be caused by:

Infection

Autoimmune disease

Neuromuscular disease

Radiation treatment

Diabetes

Eating disorders like bulimia and anorexia may cause gastroparesis, but digestive function will typically return to normal once food intake returns to normal.

Medication may cause similar symptoms, but they are usually only temporary.

Diabetes is one particularly big risk factor for this digestive condition. Long-term diabetes causes abnormalities in the nervous system, which can manifest as numbness and tingling in the fingertips or affect the nervous system in your bowels, says Marrero. High blood glucose, a problem with diabetics, can eventually weaken the vagus nerve.

What causes gastroparesis?

While the exact cause of gastroparesis isn't known, it's thought to have something to do with disrupted nerve signals in the stomach. It's believed that when the nerves to the stomach become affected by a variety of factors, food can move through it too slowly. Other problems such as the stomach being overly sensitive to signals from the nervous system and the stomach not being able to react to a meal are believed to also have a role in this condition.

Most types of gastroparesis fit into one of these categories:

idiopathic, or unknown

diabetes-related

postsurgical

Nearly 36 percent of gastroparesis cases aren't linked to an identifiable cause. This is known as idiopathic. Many times this condition occurs after a viral illness, but it's not fully understood.

A common cause of damage to the nervous system that affects the digestion is diabetes, specifically diabetes that isn't well-controlled. High blood sugar can damage nerves over time.

Surgeries that involve the stomach or other digestive organs can also change signals to the stomach. About 13 percent of people with gastroparesis have the type known as postsurgical.

Who's at risk for developing gastroparesis?

Other health conditions are also associated with gastroparesis but are less common. These include:

viral infections

some cancers

cystic fibrosis

Parkinson's disease

autoimmune diseases

amyloidosis, a condition that causes an abnormal protein buildup in organs

medications that make the stomach empty more slowly

thyroid disorders.

What are the symptoms of gastroparesis?

The symptoms of gastroparesis can range from mild to severe. They occur more often in some people than others.

The symptoms of gastroparesis can include:

upper abdominal pain

nausea

vomiting

malnutrition

unintended weight loss

Heartburn or gastroesophageal reflux disease (GERD)

Upset stomach

Vomiting/Throwing up undigested food

A feeling of fullness quickly when you eat

Bloating

Trouble controlling blood sugar

Belly pain

Other causes of gastroparesis include:

Injury to your vagus nerve from surgery

A lack of thyroid hormone (hypothyroidism)

Viral stomach infections (gastroenteritis)

Medications such as narcotics and some antidepressants

Parkinson's disease

Multiple sclerosis

Rare conditions such as amyloidosis (deposits of protein fibers in tissues and organs) and scleroderma (a connective tissue disorder that affects your skin, blood vessels, skeletal muscles, and internal organs)

Gastroparesis Diagnosis

Your doctor will perform a physical exam and ask you questions about your medical history. In order to rule out other possible causes of your symptoms, your doctor will probably want to run some tests. These might include

Carbon breath test. In this test, carbon dioxide production is tracked through the digestive system.

Blood tests. These can spot dehydration, malnutrition, infection, or blood sugar problems.

Barium X-ray. You'll drink a liquid (barium), which coats your esophagus, stomach, and small intestine and shows up on an X-ray. This is also known as an upper GI (gastrointestinal) series or a barium swallow.

Radioisotope gastric-emptying scan (gastric scintigraphy). Your doctor will give you food that contains a very small amount of something radioactive. Then, you lie under a scanning machine. If more than 10% of food is still in your stomach 4 hours after eating, you have gastroparesis.

Gastric emptying breath tests (13C-GEBTs). This is a non-radioactive test that measures how fast your stomach empties after you eat a meal that has a chemical element called the 13C isotope added to it.

Gastric manometry. Your doctor passes a thin tube through your mouth and into your stomach to check electrical and muscular activity, and to figure out how fast you're digesting.

Electrogastrography. This measures electrical activity in your stomach using electrodes on your skin.

The smart pill. You swallow a tiny electronic device that sends information about how fast it's traveling as it moves through your digestive system.

Ultrasound. This imaging test uses sound waves to create pictures of your organs. Your doctor may use it to rule out other diseases.

Upper endoscopy. Your doctor passes a thin tube called an endoscope down your esophagus to look at the lining of your stomach.

How is gastroparesis treated?

If your gastroparesis is caused by a condition like diabetes, the first step is to improve control of that underlying condition. After that, your doctor may recommend medications, diet changes, and even surgery in some cases.

Medication

Your doctor may prescribe one or more medications to treat your gastroparesis.

Medications to control nausea and vomiting caused by gastroparesis can include:

prochlorperazine (Compro)

ondansetron (Zofran)

promethazine (Phenergan)

Other medications stimulate the stomach muscles and help with digestion. These include:

metoclopramide (Reglan)

erythromycin (EES)

domperidone (Motilin)

However, these drugs can cause side effects. Talk with your doctor to weigh the pros and cons of each medication to find out which one is right for you.

Surgery

If your malnutrition or vomiting remains an issue even with the use of medications, your doctor may decide that surgery on your stomach is necessary. The goal of surgery for gastroparesis is to help your stomach empty more effectively.

A stomach stimulator known as a GES (gastric electrical stimulator) can be implanted into the stomach. This device is FDA approved for individuals who don't respond to medications. Studies have shown that in the first year after this surgery, up to 97 percent of people with a GES have less nausea and vomiting and are able to gain weight. The device may also improve life expectancy related to gastroparesis.

Diet changes

Seeing a dietitian — an expert on food and nutrition — is a common part of treatment for gastroparesis. A dietitian can suggest foods that your body can digest more easily, allowing your body to absorb more nutrients. Your dietitian might make suggestions to you, such as:

eat four to six meals per day

drink high-calorie liquids

limit alcohol and carbonated beverages

take a daily multivitamin, if tolerated

limit certain meats and dairy

eat well-cooked vegetables and fruit to lower the amount of fiber they contain

eat mostly low-fat foods

avoid foods that have a lot of fiber, like broccoli and oranges ensure there's adequate time after meals before lying down for bed substitute solid foods for pureed or liquid foods

If you have a severe case of gastroparesis, you might not be able to eat solid foods and drink liquids. In this case, you may need a feeding tube until your condition improves.

Quitting cigarette smoking can also be beneficial to your overall condition.

Experimental treatment options

Botulinum toxin type A

Botulinum toxin type A is a toxin that reduces muscle activity. It's been studied in gastroparesis and other gastrointestinal tract disorders.

Injection of the medication into the pyloric sphincter muscle improved this condition in some studies. However, due to contradictory results and the small size of most studies, scientists state that more research is needed before it can be recommended.

Vagal nerve stimulation

The vagus nerve is important to digestion. In 2018, research is underway to study the use of vagal nerve stimulation for people with gastroparesis. This study is looking at the effectiveness of self-administered nerve stimulation twice a day.

The hope is that vagal nerve stimulation will help reduce inflammation and nerve problems associated with gastroparesis.

What are the complications of gastroparesis?

The symptoms associated with gastroparesis, such as vomiting and decreased appetite, can cause dehydration and malnutrition. Dehydration and malnutrition can cause numerous problems, including:

electrolyte imbalances

decreased blood pressure

increased heartbeat

rapid breathing

decreased urine output

a weakened immune system

poor wound healing

muscle weakness

Problems might happen:

When you can't keep fluids down, and you can become dehydrated

If your body can't get the nutrients it needs, you may become malnourished.

If food stays in your stomach too long and ferments, which can lead to the growth of bacteria

When food hardens into a solid lump called a bezoar. This can block food from passing into your small intestine.

If you have diabetes. Your blood sugar levels may rise when food finally leaves your stomach and enters your small intestine. Gastroparesis makes it harder to control your blood sugar.

Since gastroparesis causes food to stay in the stomach for too long, it can also cause an overgrowth of bacteria.

The food can also harden into masses called bezoars that cause nausea, vomiting, and obstruction in the stomach

Managing blood glucose levels is essential for people with diabetes. Gastroparesis can make it harder to manage those levels.

Outlook

If you suspect you have gastroparesis, talk to your doctor. They'll do a thorough exam before diagnosing the condition. If you do have gastroparesis, work with your doctor to develop a treatment plan based on your particular health needs.

Surgery for gastroparesis

Gastroparesis patients who still have nausea and vomiting even after taking medications may benefit from surgery. One type of surgery for gastroparesis is gastric electrical stimulation, which is a treatment that sends mild electric shocks to the stomach muscles. In this procedure, the doctor inserts a small device called a gastric stimulator into the abdomen. The stimulator has two leads that are attached to the stomach and provide the mild electric shocks, which help control vomiting. The strength of the electric shocks can be adjusted by the doctor. The device runs on a battery that lasts up to 10 years.

Another surgery to relieve gastroparesis symptoms is gastric bypass, in which a small pouch is created from the top part of the stomach. The small intestine is divided in half and the lower end is attached directly to the small stomach pouch. This limits the amount of food the patient can eat. This surgery is more effective for an obese diabetic patient than either medication or a gastric stimulator.

Are there any other treatments for gastroparesis?

A newer treatment for gastroparesis is called per oral pyloromyotomy (POP). This is a nonsurgical procedure in which the doctor inserts an endoscope (a long, thin, flexible instrument) into the patient's mouth and advances it to the stomach. The doctor then cuts the pylorus, the valve that empties the stomach, which allows food to move from the stomach to the small intestine more easily.

In a severe case of gastroparesis, your doctor may decide you would benefit from a feeding tube, or jejunostomy tube. The tube is inserted in a surgical procedure through your abdomen into your small intestine. To feed yourself, you put nutrients into the tube, which go directly into your small intestine; this way, they go around the stomach and get into your bloodstream more quickly. The jejunostomy tube is usually a temporary measure.

Another treatment option is intravenous, or parenteral, nutrition. This is a feeding method in which nutrients go directly into your bloodstream through a catheter placed into a vein in your chest. Like a jejunostomy tube, parenteral nutrition is meant to be a temporary measure for a severe case of gastroparesis.

Should I change my diet if I have gastroparesis?

One of the best ways to help control the symptoms of gastroparesis is to change your daily eating habits. For instance, instead of three meals a day, you can eat six small meals. In this way, there is less food in your stomach; you won't feel as full, and it will be easier for the food to leave your stomach.

Another important factor is the texture of food; liquids and low residue are encouraged (for example, you should eat applesauce instead of whole apples with intact skins).

You should also avoid foods that are high in fat (which can slow down digestion) and fiber (which is difficult to digest).

Foods to eat if you have gastroparesis

If you have gastroparesis, it's important to focus on getting the nutrition that you need while eating small, frequent meals that are low in fat and easy to digest.

The staples of this kind of diet include high-protein foods (such as eggs and nut butter) and easy-to-digest vegetables (such as cooked zucchini).

If the food is easy to chew and swallow, that's a good indication that you'll have an easier time digesting it.

Here's a list of suggested foods that may help keep your gastroparesis in check:

eggs

peanut butter

bananas

breads, hot cereals, and crackers

fruit juice

vegetable juice (spinach, kale, carrots)

fruit purees

Foods to avoid if you have gastroparesis

If you currently have gastroparesis symptoms, you should be aware of what foods to avoid.

As a general rule, foods that are high in saturated fat or fiber should only be eaten in small amounts.

Here's a list of foods that might make your gastroparesis discomfort worse:

carbonated beverages

alcohol

beans and legumes

corn

seeds and nuts

broccoli and cauliflower

cheese

heavy cream

excess oil or butter

Gastroparesis recovery diet

When you're recovering from gastroparesis, you might need to be on a multiphase diet that gradually reintroduces solid foods.

The Gastroparesis Patient Association for Cures and Treatments (G-PACT) describes the three phases of this diet in their diet guidelines.

The three phases are as follows:

First phase: You're limited mostly to broth or bullion soups, as well as blended vegetable juice.

Second phase: You may work up to soups that contain crackers and noodles, as well as cheese and peanut butter.

Third phase: You're allowed to have most soft, easy-to-chew starches as well as softer protein sources such as poultry and fish.

During all phases of this recovery diet, you need to avoid red meat and high-fiber vegetables because they take longer to digest.

Diet tips

When you have gastroparesis, you should be mindful of how often and in what order you consume foods. It's recommended you eat small meals, five to eight times per day.

Chew your food well before swallowing it. Eat nutritious foods first to keep from becoming full from foods that don't fuel your body.

While recovering from gastroparesis, consider taking a multivitamin supplement so that you can still get the nutrition you need. If weight loss has been a symptom of your gastroparesis, aim for a minimum of 1,500 calories a day as you begin your recovery.

Nutritional drinks such as yogurt smoothies, fruit and vegetable smoothies, liquid meal replacement shakes, and protein shakes are easy-to-digest liquids that can help with this.

Drink plenty of water so that your digestive system doesn't get dehydrated.

Avoid alcohol when you have gastroparesis symptoms, as alcohol can dehydrate or constipate you further — not to mention deplete your body of nutrition.

Gastroparesis Recovery Diet Recipes

Your food options might feel limited when you have gastroparesis, but you can still enjoy some delicious recipes.

Peach banana smoothies and green smoothies with peanut butter contain the nutrition you need and taste great.

For savory options, garlic mashed potatoes and gastroparesis-friendly vegetable soup have little fiber but lots of taste.

Best Diet for Gastroparesis

While there is no one best diet for gastroparesis, there are specific strategies that help support digestion and stomach motility.

These four factors impact stomach emptying rate and should be considered when developing a diet for gastroparesis:

Liquids: Thin liquids like water, broth and juices rapidly empty the stomach. They require little to no digestion and use the effect of gravity to move down to the small intestine. Thicker liquids such as pureed soups or smoothies empty at a slower rate.

Solids: Solid food requires more work for the stomach, which needs to break it down to pass into the small intestine. This process slows stomach emptying.

Nutrient Composition: Fiber and fat-rich foods and oils also take longer to empty from the stomach. Carbohydrates can pass through the quickest, followed by proteins.

Food Temperature: The temperature of food when it enters the stomach affects when it leaves. Hot meals and beverages will exit the stomach faster than cool foods and liquids.

The Three-Phased Diet Approach

With these concepts in mind, a three-phased diet approach is often recommended for those with gastroparesis.

1 – Phase One:

Lasting less than three days, the first phase consists of thin liquids and saltine crackers.

Calories are inadequate, typically under 800 daily, so this phase should last no longer than three days, unless additional nutrition support is included.

Gatorade, ginger ale and other sodas, broths, juices and water are consumed. Since you'll only be meeting your fluid and electrolyte needs these days, it's important to follow this phase under the supervision of your healthcare provider.

2 – Phase Two:

Fat intake progressively increases up to 40 grams daily. Calories may still be less than adequate, but should slowly increase as tolerated.

This phase typically lasts 4-6 weeks, but depends on the degree of improvement in your symptoms.

Food choices may include fat-free dairy, thicker soups, grains (not whole grains), eggs, peanut butter (limit to two tablespoons), fruit and vegetable juices, canned fruits, peeled and well-cooked veggies, and low-fat desserts (puddings, frozen yogurt, gelatin, popsicles, etc.).

3 – Phase Three:

Calorie and fat intake increases up to 50 grams daily.

This is considered a maintenance phase, and should still be monitored and modified under the care of your healthcare professional.

Continue focusing on a low-fiber diet and eating smaller meals spaced throughout the day. Tailor the diet to meet your specific nutritional needs.

In case your needs are not fully met on this plan, talk to your healthcare provider about using a multivitamin or mineral supplement. In severe cases, short- or long-term enteral (feeding-tube) or parenteral (intravenous) nutrition may be required.

Essential Long-Term Diet Tips

Try these simple diet tips to keep symptoms of gastroparesis at bay:

Eat Small, Frequent Meals: This allows you to meet your calorie and nutrient needs without overfilling the stomach. You'll feel less bloated and uncomfortable with smaller portions of food.

Chew Your Food Well: This will help relieve your stomach from overworking to break down food. When food is broken down by your teeth it also has time to mix with salivary enzymes to "pre-digest" before being swallowed.

Take Advantage of Gravity: By remaining upright and going for a light walk after eating, your food is more likely to be pulled down into the small intestine to continue digesting. Avoid eating too late at night and/or taking naps or reclining in a chair after eating.

Consider Liquid-Meal Replacements: Products like Ensure and Boost or homemade protein shakes or smoothies can help you meet your calorie needs.

Avoid High-Fat Foods: Skip the fried foods, high-fat meats, full-fat dairy and baked goods. Instead, enjoy limited amounts of healthy fats like extra virgin olive oil, avocado, nut or seed butters and fatty fish.

Limit Fiber Intake: Avoid high fiber foods like whole grains and legumes (e.g. beans, peas, lentils), as well as the skins and seeds of fruits and veggies. This helps reduce the risk of developing bezoars, which can cause stomach blockages.

Enjoy Your Nuts & Seeds Pureed: Nut and seed butters are more easily digested than whole nuts and seeds. But don't overdo these if you're trying to lose weight—they're still high in fat and therefore high in calories.

Choose Nutrient-Dense Foods: Since every calorie counts, don't waste them on junk food. Choose 100% juice, low-fat dairy products (e.g. yogurt, cheese, milk), peeled fruits and vegetables, lean meats and seafood. Occasional intake of treats is okay, focusing on lower fat options like rice krispy treats, low fat pudding and angel food cake.

Avoid Alcoholic Spirits: Drinks like vodka, rum, tequila, etc., can slow gastric motility (5).

Summary: While there's not one best diet for gastroparesis, you should aim to eat slowly and enjoy small frequent meals. You must also choose nutrient-rich foods that are low in fat and fiber.

Sample Gastroparesis Diet Plan

Sample Meal Plan & RecipesYour maintenance diet for gastroparesis may include the following foods:

Fruits & Vegetables: baby food, homemade fruit and vegetable purees, canned and/or frozen fruits and vegetables, 100% fruit or vegetable juice, smoothies, pureed low-fat vegetable soups, well-cooked and de-skinned vegetable

Proteins: low-fat or fat-free milk, low-fat or fat-free yogurt, low-fat or fat-free cheese, lean (not skin, fat-trimmed) meat and poultry, ground lean meats, eggs or egg whites, fish, shellfish, limited creamy nut/seed butters

Starches: white rices, white breads, mashed potatoes (skin removed), pastas, noodles, crackers, cereals (avoid whole grains)

Oils: any as long as they are limited overall (under 50 grams of fat daily)

Sample 3-Day Diet Plan

Below is a sample meal plan you may follow, though it should be adjusted for your specific calorie and nutrient needs.

Day One:

Breakfast: 1 cup of puffed rice cereal with skim milk and sliced ripe bananas

Snack 1: apple sauce

Lunch: chicken noodle soup, 6 saltine crackers

Snack 2: saltine crackers with a thin layer of almond butter

Dinner: Chinese stir fry with white rice, tofu, well-cooked veggies (carrots, onions, snow peas) with soy sauce

Snack 3: low-fat pudding cup

Day Two:

Breakfast: 2 slices of white toast lightly topped with peanut butter and strawberry jam, Ensure/Boost shake

Snack 1: canned peaches

Lunch: egg noodles tossed with steamed shrimp and stewed tomatoes

Snack 2: green juice, pretzels

Dinner: roasted vegetable soup, side of turkey

Snack 3: frozen yogurt popsicle

Day Three:

Breakfast: scrambled egg whites with sauteed spinach and pinch of low-fat cheddar cheese, side of canned pineapple chunks

Snack 1: protein shake

Lunch: smoothie with low-fat yogurt, frozen berries, orange juice, protein powder

Snack 2: vegetable soup

Dinner: baked salmon with side of mashed potatoes

Snack 3: cream of wheat with honey and spoonful of peanut butter

Gastroparesis and the Low FODMAP Diet

If you have implemented all the above strategies with little success, there is one other option.

The main symptoms of gastroparesis (particularly bloating) greatly overlap with those of irritable bowel syndrome (IBS) and small intestinal bacterial overgrowth (SIBO). Both these conditions can be treated with a low FODMAP diet, among other things.

In fact, there is evidence that those with gastroparesis are much more likely to have or develop SIBO.

Given the overlap, some doctors and even patients have begun to wonder if minimizing FODMAPs will also help with this condition. I was unable to find any scientific literature yet, but theoretically it makes sense that it would help.

It's often due to conditions that impair the nerve and muscle functioning of the stomach. While medical treatments are available, dietary change is the initial and ideal option.

The best diet for gastroparesis typically depends on the severity of the condition. Initially you may consider trying the three-phased gastroparesis diet, which starts with clear liquids, and then slowly progresses to a maintenance plan of nutrient-rich foods.

When symptoms are acting up, it's generally best to eat smaller meals, limit fiber, choose low-fat options and consider liquid meal replacements as needed. You can also consider trialling a low FODMAP diet if nothing else has helped.

Making these simple changes to the way you eat can go a long way to successfully managing gastroparesis.

GLUTEN FREE RECIPES

Gluten free Appetizers

Lion's Den Lobster Fritters (Gluten Free)
Rated as 5 out of 5 Stars

Ingredients

1 quart vegetable oil for frying, 1 cup of gluten free pancake mix (such as Arrowhead Mills®), 1/2 cup of finely chopped onions, 1/2 cup of finely chopped celery, 1/2 cup of unsweetened shredded coconut, 1/2 cup of crushed gluten free crackers (such as Glutino), 1 lobster tail, shelled, cleaned, and chopped, 1 table spoon seafood seasoning (such as Old Bay), 1 ¼ of a teaspoon of baking powder, 1 tea spoon of salt, 1 tea spoon of ground black pepper, 2 eggs, 1/2 cup of evaporated milk, 1 tablespoon garlic butter melted.

Directions:

Heat oil in a large pot or deep fryer to 365 degrees F (185 degrees C).

Combine gluten free pancake mix, onions, celery, coconut, gluten free crackers, lobster meat, seafood seasoning, baking powder, salt, and ground black pepper in a bowl.

Combine eggs, evaporated milk, and butter in a separate bowl.

Stir egg mixture into dry mixture to form a batter.

Drop batter by rounded tablespoons into hot oil and fry until golden brown, about 3 minutes.

Remove and drain fritters on a rack.

Cook's note:

This makes a big batch. Lobster meat can be replaced with any seafood successfully. I mix together Hellman's Mayo, Sweet Baby Ray's BBQ sauce, and Heinz Ketchup to taste to serve alongside. My hubby is the pickiest eater I know, and he said these were amazing. I don't disagree.

Gluten-Free Nuts and Seeds Clusters
Rated as 4.5 out of 5 Stars

Ingredients

1 cup of rolled oats, 3/4 cup of oat flour, 1/4 cup of sesame seeds, 1/4 cup of cornstarch, 1/4 cup of quinoa, 1/4 cup of flaked coconut, 1/4 cup of flax seed meal, 1/4 cup of chia seeds, 1/4 cup walnuts, finely chopped, 1/4 cup of raisins finely chopped, 1/4 cup of sunflower seeds, finely chopped, 1/4 cup of white chocolate chips, finely chopped, 1/2 tea spoon ground cinnamon, 1/2 teaspoon of salt, 1 cup of honey, 2/3 cup of applesauce, 1/2 cup of coconut oil, melted, 1 egg, 2 teaspoons of vanilla extract.

Directions

Preheat oven to 350 degrees F (175 degrees C). Grease a miniature muffin tin.

Combine oats, oat flour, sesame seeds, cornstarch, quinoa, coconut, flax meal, chia seeds, walnuts, raisins, sunflower seeds, white chocolate chips, cinnamon, and salt in a large bowl.

Whisk honey, applesauce, coconut oil, egg, and vanilla extract together in a separate bowl; stir into oats mixture. Scoop mixture into the prepared muffin tin, pressing gently to fit into each muffin cup.

Bake in the preheated oven until cooked through and lightly browned, 15 to 20 minutes.

Cook's Notes:

Be sure the oats are gluten-free if you are sensitive to gluten.

Replace raisins with any dried fruit, such as dried cranberries or mangoes.

If you don't have a mini muffin pan, simply use a tablespoon to scoop out each portion and shape it into a ball before placing it on a baking sheet.

Nutrition Facts

Per Serving: 92 calories; 4.9 g fat; 11.7 g carbohydrates; 1.4 g protein; 4 mg cholesterol; 28 mg sodium.

Keto Sausage Balls

Rating: 4.18 stars

Quick and simple, keto and gluten free. Perfect Game Day snack! I like this recipe best with hot sausage for a little kick, but you can make it to your preference. Serve plain or with honey mustard.

Ingredient Checklist

1 pound spicy ground pork sausage

½ (8 ounce) package cream cheese, at room temperature

½ cup shredded sharp Cheddar cheese

½ cup grated Parmesan cheese

1 tablespoon Dijon mustard

½ teaspoon garlic powder

¼ teaspoon salt

Directions

Step 1

Preheat the oven to 350 degrees F (175 degrees C). Line a baking sheet with parchment paper.

Step 2

Combine sausage, cream cheese, Cheddar cheese, Parmesan cheese, mustard, garlic powder, and salt in a large bowl. Mix gently until just combined. Roll heaping tablespoonfuls of the pork mixture into balls. Place on the prepared baking sheet.

Step 3

Bake in the preheated oven until golden brown, 30 to 35 minutes. Place on a paper towel-lined plate to soak up excess grease. Serve immediately.

Nutrition Facts

Per Serving:

101 calories; 8.3 g total fat; 26 mg cholesterol; 285 mg sodium. 0.8 g carbohydrates; 5.6 g protein;

Lasagna-Stuffed Mushrooms
Rated as 4.41 out of 5 Stars

Ingredients

1/4 pound lean ground beef1/2 cup fat-free small curd cottage cheese1 egg1 tablespoon finely chopped green onion1 tablespoon chopped fresh parsleysalt and black pepper to taste1/4 cup prepared pasta sauce, divided6 large fresh mushrooms, or more as needed, stems removed1/4 cup shredded mozzarella cheese, divided.

Directions

Preheat oven to 375 degrees F (190 degrees C). Spray an 8x8-inch baking dish with cooking spray.

Cook and stir the ground beef in a skillet over medium heat, breaking it apart as it cooks, until the meat is no longer pink, about 10 minutes. Mix together the cottage cheese, egg, green onion, parsley, and salt and pepper in a bowl until the mixture is well combined. Stir in the cooked ground beef.

Place the mushrooms, hollow sides up, close together in the prepared baking dish. Spoon about 1 tablespoon of the cheese filling into the cavity of each mushroom, and allow remaining filling to overflow between mushrooms.

Bake in the preheated oven until the cheese filling is set, about 15 minutes. Remove dish from oven, and spread the pasta sauce evenly over the mushrooms. Sprinkle an even layer of mozzarella cheese over the sauce, return the dish to the oven, and broil until the cheese is bubbling and beginning to brown, about 5 more minutes. Let the mushrooms stand 5 minutes before serving.

Nutrition Facts

Per Serving: 263 calories; 12.7 g fat; 9.9 g carbohydrates; 26.8 g protein; 142 mg cholesterol; 509 mg sodium

Fava Bean Breakfast Spread
Rated as 4.6 out of 5 Stars

Ingredients

1 (15 ounce) can of fava beans, 1 ½ tablespoons of olive oil, 1 large onion, chopped, 1 large tomato, diced, 1 tea spoon of ground cumin, 1/4 cup of chopped fresh parsley, 1/4 cup of fresh lemon, juice salt and pepper to taste, ground red pepper, to taste.

Directions

Pour the beans into a pot and bring to a boil. Mix them well and add onion, tomato, olive oil, cumin, parsley, lemon juice, salt, pepper, and red pepper. Bring the mixture back to a boil, then reduce the heat to medium. Let the mixture cook 5 minutes. Serve warm with grilled pita.

Nutrition Facts

Per Serving: 101 calories; 3.7 g fat; 13.6 g carbohydrates; 4.6 g protein; 0 mg cholesterol; 322 mg sodium.

Scalloped Potatoes for the BBQ

Ingredient Checklist

4 red potatoes, thinly sliced

1 large onion, chopped

4 cloves of garlic, chopped

¼ cup of chopped fresh basil

¼ cup of butter, cubed

salt and pepper to taste

Directions Checklist

Step 1

Preheat grill for medium heat.

Step 2

Layer sliced potatoes on aluminum foil with the onion, garlic, basil, and butter. Season with salt and pepper. Fold foil around the potatoes to make a packet.

Step 3

Place potato packet on heated grill over indirect heat, and cook for 30 minutes, or until potatoes are tender. Turn over packet halfway through cooking.

Crab Stuffed Mushrooms

Ingredients

1 pound of fresh mushrooms, 7 ounces of crabmeat, 5 green onions thinly sliced, 1/4 tea spoon of dried thyme, 1/4 tea spoon of dried oregano, 1/4 tea spoon of ground savory, ground black pepper to taste, 1/4 cup of grated Parmesan cheese, 1/3 cup of mayonnaise, 3 table spoons of grated Parmesan cheese, 1/4 tea spoon of paprika.

Directions

Preheat the oven to 350 degrees F (175 degrees C).

In a medium bowl, combine crabmeat, green onions, herbs, and pepper. Mix in mayonnaise and 1/4 cup Parmesan cheese until well combined. Refrigerate filling until ready for use. Watch Now

Wipe the mushrooms clean with a damp towel. Remove stems. Spoon out the gills and the base of the stem, making deep cups. Discard gills and stems. Fill the mushroom caps with rounded teaspoonfuls of filling, and place them in an ungreased shallow baking dish. Sprinkle tops with Parmesan and paprika.

Bake for 15 minutes. Remove from oven, and serve immediately!

Nutrition Facts

Per Serving: 167 calories; 12.1 g fat; 4.2 g carbohydrates; 11.7 g protein; 39 mg cholesterol; 275 mg sodium.

Bacon and Date Appetizer

Ingredient Checklist:

1 (8 ounce) package pitted dates

4 ounces of almonds

1 pound of sliced bacon

Directions Checklist

Step 1

Preheat the broiler.

Step 2

Slit dates. Place one almond inside each date. Wrap dates with bacon, using toothpicks to hold them together.

Step 3

Broil 10 minutes, or until bacon is evenly brown and crisp.

Buffalo Cauliflower

Ingredients:

olive oil cooking spray, 3/4 cup of gluten-free baking flour (such as Premium Gold® Flax and Ancient Grains All-Purpose Flour), 1 cup of water, 1/2 tea spoon of garlic powder or to taste, salt and ground black pepper to taste, 2 heads of cauliflower, cut into bite-size pieces, 2 table spoons of butter, 1/2 cup of hot pepper sauce (such as Frank's RedHot®) and 1 tea spoon of honey.

Directions

Preheat oven to 450 degrees F (230 degrees C). Lightly grease a baking sheet with cooking spray.

Mix flour, water, garlic powder, salt, and pepper together in a bowl using a whisk until batter is smooth and somewhat runny. Add cauliflower to batter and mix until cauliflower is coated; spread onto the baking sheet.

Bake in the preheated oven until lightly browned, 20 to 25 minutes. Watch

Melt butter in a saucepan over medium heat. Remove saucepan from heat and stir hot pepper sauce and honey into butter until smooth. Brush hot sauce mixture over each cauliflower piece, repeating brushing until all the hot sauce mixture is used. Watch Now

Bake in the oven until cauliflower is browned, about 10 minutes. Remove baking sheet from oven and allow the cauliflower to cool 10 to 15 minutes.

Cook's Note:

Gluten-free flour uses less liquid than wheat flour. You may have to adjust the liquid based on the flour you are using. All-purpose flour can be used in place of gluten-free if desired.

Low-Carb Almond Garlic Crackers
Ingredients

1/2 cup of almond meal, 1/2 cup of ground flax seed, 1/2 cup of water, 1/3 cup of shredded Parmesan cheese, 1 teaspoon of garlic powder, 1/2 tea spoon of salt.

Directions

Preheat oven to 400 degrees F (200 degrees C). Line a baking sheet with parchment paper.

Mix almond meal, ground flax seed, water, Parmesan cheese, garlic powder, and salt together in a bowl. Set aside until water is absorbed and dough holds together, 3 to 5 minutes.

Put dough on the prepared baking sheet and top with waxed paper or plastic wrap. Flatten the dough to 1/8-inch thick using a rolling pin or your hands. Remove waxed paper. Score the dough with a knife to make indentations of where you will break the crackers apart.

Bake in the preheated oven until golden brown, about 15 minutes. Remove baking sheet from oven and cool crackers to room temperature, at least 30 minutes; break into individual crackers.

Nutrition Facts

Per Serving: 72 calories; 5.7 g fat; 3.1 g carbohydrates; 3.1 g protein; 2 mg cholesterol; 135 mg sodium. Full nutrition

GLUTEN FREE BREAKFAST AND BRUNCH RECIPES

Momma's Potatoes
Rated as 4.22 out of 5 Stars

Ingredients

8 Yukon Gold potatoes, quartered, 1 table spoon of dried rosemary, 1/4 cup of olive oil, salt and pepper to taste.

Directions

Preheat oven to 350 degrees F (175 degrees C).

In a large bowl, combine the potatoes, rosemary, oil, salt and pepper. Toss well to coat.

Spread evenly onto cookie sheet and bake in preheated oven for 30 minutes.

Nutrition Facts

Per Serving: 450 calories; 14 g fat; 74.9 g carbohydrates; 8.6 g protein; 0 mg cholesterol; 26 mg sodium

Feta Eggs

Rated as 4.58 out of 5 Stars

Ingredients

1 table spoon of butter, 1/4 cup of chopped onion, 4 eggs beaten, 1/4 cup of chopped tomatoes, 2 table spoons, crumbled feta cheese salt and pepper to taste.

Directions

Melt butter in a skillet over medium heat. Saute onions until translucent. Pour in eggs. Cook, stirring occasionally to scramble. When eggs appear almost done, stir in chopped tomatoes and feta cheese, and season with salt and pepper. Cook until cheese is melted.

Nutrition Facts

Per Serving: 116 calories; 8.9 g fat; 2 g carbohydrates; 7.2 g protein; 198 mg cholesterol; 435 mg sodium

Bacon Breakfast Casserole (Gluten Free)
Rating: 4.75 stars

This is a simple recipe, easy to make. Really nice when you have company over in the morning. Get it ready, pop it in the oven and you have time to socialize while it's cooking! I cut this recipe in half and place it in a pie plate and bake uncovered for 45 minutes for breakfast for a smaller family; it tastes very much like a crustless quiche and my husband loves it!

Ingredient Checklist

1 pound of bacon

2 cups of milk

8 eggs

1 tea spoon of seasoned salt

1 tea spoon of ground black pepper

2 cups of shredded Cheddar cheese

1 onion, chopped

1 green bell pepper, chopped

3 red potatoes, thinly sliced

5 mushrooms, sliced

Directions Checklist

Step 1

Place bacon in a large skillet and cook over medium-high heat, turning occasionally, until evenly browned, about 10 minutes. Drain bacon slices on paper towels, reserving 1 tablespoon bacon grease. Crumble bacon into pieces.

Step 2

Preheat oven to 350 degrees F (175 degrees C). Grease a 9x13-inch casserole dish with reserved bacon grease.

Step 3

Place milk, eggs, seasoned salt, and black pepper in the bowl of a stand mixer fitted with a paddle attachment. Beat on medium speed until smooth and pale, about 5 minutes. Add bacon pieces, Cheddar cheese, onion, and green bell pepper; beat until combined, about 1 1/2 minutes more.

Step 4

Layer potato slices in the bottom of the casserole dish. Pour egg mixture over potatoes. Arrange sliced mushrooms on top. Cover casserole with aluminum foil.

Step 5

Bake in the preheated oven, about 35 minutes. Remove aluminum foil and bake until eggs are set, about 30 minutes more.

Nutrition Facts

Per Serving:

276 calories; 18.8 g total fat; 193 mg cholesterol; 655 mg sodium. 8.1 g carbohydrates; 18.7 g protein

Berry Good Smoothie II

Rated as 3.8 out of 5 Stars

Ingredients

1 nectarine, pitted, 3/4 cup of strawberries, hulled, 3/4 cup of blueberries, rinsed and drained, 1/3 cup of non-fat dry milk powder and 1 cup of crushed ice.

Directions

In a blender combine nectarine, strawberries, blueberries, milk powder and crushed ice. Blend until smooth. pour into glasses and serve.

Nutrition Facts

Per Serving: 151 calories; 0.7 g fat; 29.6 g carbohydrates; 8.7 g protein; 4 mg cholesterol; 110 mg sodium

Sweet Potato and Banana Pancakes

Rated as 4.91 out of 5 Stars

Delicious, moist, protein-rich, and filling pancakes. Gluten-free and paleo-friendly. Enjoy with your favorite toppings. I like peanut butter with berries on mine!"

Ingredients:

1 large sweet potato, 1 ½ cups of bananas, 6 eggs, 1/4 teaspoon of vanilla extract, 1/3 cup of coconut flour, 1/3 cup of almond flour, 1 tea spoon of baking powder, 1 tea spoon of ground cinnamon.

Directions:

Preheat oven to 350 degrees F (175 degrees C). Place sweet potato in a baking dish.

Bake in the preheated oven until flesh is easily punctured with a fork, 45 minutes to 1 hour. Allow sweet potato to cool until easily handled; peel.

Mash sweet potato and bananas together in a bowl using a fork or electric mixer until smooth; add eggs and vanilla extract and mix well.

Whisk coconut flour, almond flour, baking powder, and cinnamon together in a separate bowl; stir into sweet potato mixture until batter is well combined and thick.

Heat a lightly oiled griddle over medium heat. Drop about 1/4 cup of batter onto the griddle and cook until bubbles form and the edges are dry, 4 to 5 minutes. Flip and flatten pancake with spatula and cook until browned on the other side, 3 to 5 minutes. Repeat with remaining batter.

Nutrition Facts

Per Serving: 226 calories; 6.2 g fat; 34.8 g carbohydrates; 9.7 g protein; 223 mg cholesterol; 232 mg sodium

Mango Coconut Chia Pudding
Rated as 4.67 out of 5 Stars

"This makes the perfect breakfast or midday snack. Move over, silly little chia pets, chia seeds are loaded with nutrients and meant to be eaten!"

Ingredients

1 mango, peeled and diced, 2/3 cup of unsweetened coconut milk beverage (such as Silk®), 1 tablespoon of maple syrup. 2 table spoons of chia seeds, 2 table spoons of unsweetened coconut flakes (such as Bob's Red Mill®), divided.

Directions

Mash half of the mango in a bowl with a fork or puree in a food processor to desired consistency.

Whisk coconut milk beverage and maple syrup into the mashed mango; stir in chia seeds and 1 tablespoon coconut flakes. Cover and refrigerate until thickened, at least 1 hour.

Divide pudding between 2 bowls and top with diced mango and remaining coconut flakes.

Nutrition Facts

Per Serving: 210 calories; 9 g fat; 34.1 g carbohydrates; 2 g protein; 0 mg cholesterol; 9 mg sodium.

Country style fried Potatoes

Ingredients

1/3 cup of shortening 6 large potatoes, peeled and cubed, 1 tea spoon of salt, 1/2 tea spoon of ground black pepper, 1/2 teaspoon of garlic powder, 1/2 tea spoon of paprika.

Directions

In a large cast iron skillet, heat shortening over medium-high heat. Add potatoes and cook, stirring occasionally, until potatoes are golden brown. Season with salt, pepper, garlic powder and paprika. Serve hot.

Nutrition Facts

Per Serving: 326 calories; 11.7 g fat; 52.1 g carbohydrates; 4.8 g protein; 0 mg cholesterol; 400 mg sodium.

Delicious Gluten Free Pancakes

Ingredients

1 cup rice flour 3 table spoons tapioca flour 1/3 cup potato starch 4 table spoons dry buttermilk powder1 packet sugar substitute1 1/2 tea spoons baking powder 1/2 tea spoon baking soda 1/2 tea spoon salt 1/2 tea spoon xanthan gum 2 eggs 3 table spoons canola oil 2 cups water.

Directions

In a bowl, mix or sift together the rice flour, tapioca flour, potato starch, dry buttermilk powder, sugar substitute, baking powder, baking soda, salt, and xanthan gum. Stir in eggs, water, and oil until well blended and few lumps remain. Watch Now

Heat a large, well-oiled skillet or griddle over medium high heat. Spoon batter onto skillet and cook until bubbles begin to form. Flip, and continue cooking until golden brown on bottom. Serve immediately with condiments of your choice. Watch Now

Nutrition Facts

Per Serving: 147 calories; 5.8 g fat; 20.4 g carbohydrates; 3.1 g protein; 29 mg cholesterol; 269 mg sodium.

Sarah's Apple Sauce

Ingredients:

4 apples - peeled, cored and chopped3/4 cup water1/4 cup white sugar1/2 teaspoon ground cinnamon.

Directions:

In a saucepan, combine apples, water, sugar, and cinnamon. Cover, and cook over medium heat for 15 to 20 minutes, or until apples are soft. Allow to cool, then mash with a fork or potato masher.

Nutrition Facts

Per Serving: 121 calories; 0.2 g fat; 31.8 g carbohydrates; 0.4 g protein; 0 mg cholesterol; 3 mg sodium.

Sauteed Apples

Ingredients

1/4 cup butter 4 large tart apples - peeled, cored and sliced 1/4 inch thick of 2 tea spoons of corn starch 1/2 cup of cold water, 1/2 cup of brown sugar and 1/2 tea spoon ground cinnamon.

Directions

In a large skillet or saucepan, melt butter over medium heat; add apples. Cook, stirring constantly, until apples are almost tender, about 6 to 7 minutes.

Dissolve cornstarch in water; add to skillet. Stir in brown sugar and cinnamon. Boil for 2 minutes, stirring occasionally. Remove from heat and serve warm.

Nutrition Facts

Per Serving: 143 calories; 5.9 g fat; 24.3 g carbohydrates; 0.4 g protein; 15 mg cholesterol; 45 mg sodium.

Greek Scrambled Eggs

Ingredients:

1 table spoon of butter, 3 eggs, 1 tea spoon of water, 1/2 cup of crumbled feta cheese, salt and pepper to taste.

Directions

Heat butter in a skillet over medium-high heat. Beat eggs and water together, then pour into pan. Add feta cheese, and cook, stirring occasionally to scramble. Season with salt and pepper.

Nutrition Facts

Per Serving: 257 calories; 21.2 g fat; 2.1 g carbohydrates; 14.8 g protein; 328 mg cholesterol; 710 mg sodium. Full nutrition

GLUTEN FREE MAIN DISHES

Rump Roast Au Jus

Ingredients

1 table spoon of ground black pepper, 1 table spoon of paprika, 2 tea spoons of chili powder, 1/2 tea spoon of celery salt, 1/2 tea spoon of ground cayenne pepper, 1/2 tea spoon of garlic powder, 1/4 tea spoon of mustard powder, 1 (4 pound) rump roast and 1/2 cup of water.

Directions

10 h 10 m

In a small bowl, mix together black pepper, paprika, chili powder, celery salt, cayenne pepper, garlic powder, and mustard powder. Rub mixture over the surface of the meat. Place roast in a slow cooker, and add 1/2 cup of water.

Cover, and cook on Low for 8 to 10 hours. When meat is tender and well done, transfer roast to a serving platter. Skim fat from juices, and strain; serve with meat.

Grilled Sea Bass

Ingredients

1/4 tea spoon of garlic powder, 1/4 tea spoon of onion powder, 1/4 tea spoon of paprika, lemon pepper to taste, sea salt to taste, 2 pounds of sea bass, 3 table spoons of butter, 2 large cloves of garlic, chopped, 1 table spoon chopped, Italian flat leaf parsley and 1 ½ table spoons of extra virgin olive oil.

Directions

Preheat grill for high heat.

In a small bowl, stir together the garlic powder, onion powder, paprika, lemon pepper, and sea salt. Sprinkle seasonings onto the fish.

In a small saucepan over medium heat, melt the butter with the garlic and parsley. Remove from heat when the butter has melted, and set aside.

Lightly oil grill grate. Grill fish for 7 minutes, then turn and drizzle with butter. Continue cooking for 7 minutes, or until easily flaked with a fork. Drizzle with olive oil before serving.

Chick Pea Curry

Ingredients

2 table spoons of vegetable oil, 2 onions minced, 2 cloves of garlic minced, 2 tea spoons of fresh ginger root, finely chopped, 6 whole cloves, 2 (2 inch) sticks of cinnamon, crushed, 1 tea spoon of ground cumin, 1 tea spoon of ground coriander salt, 1 tea spoon cayenne pepper, 1 teaspoon of ground turmeric, 2 (15 ounce) cans of garbanzo beans, 1 cup of chopped fresh cilantro.

Directions

Heat oil in a large frying pan over medium heat, and fry onions until tender. Watch Now

Stir in garlic, ginger, cloves, cinnamon, cumin, coriander, salt, cayenne, and turmeric. Cook for 1 minute over medium heat, stirring constantly. Mix in garbanzo beans and their liquid. Continue to cook and stir until all ingredients are well blended and heated through. Remove from heat. Stir in cilantro just before serving, reserving 1 table spoon for garnish.

Fish Fillets Italiano

Rated as 4.43 out of 5 Stars

"Cod and haddock fillets work well for this braised dish. An extra easy and quick way to fix a superb tasting fish dish! Serve over rice."

Ingredients

2 table spoons of olive oil, 1 onion, thinly sliced, 2 cloves of garlic, minced, 1 (14.5 ounce) can of diced tomatoes, 1/2 cup of black olives, pitted and sliced, 1 table spoon of chopped fresh parsley, 1/2 cup of dry white wine, 1 pound of cod fillets.

Directions

In a large frying pan, heat oil over medium heat. Saute onions and garlic in olive oil until softened.

Stir in tomatoes, olives, parsley, and wine. Simmer for 5 minutes.

Place fillets in sauce. Simmer for about 5 more minutes, or until fish turns white.

Nutrition Facts

Per Serving: 230 calories; 9.4 g fat; 8.2 g carbohydrates; 21.2 g protein; 41 mg cholesterol; 459 mg sodium.

Rosemary Braised Lamb Shanks
Rated as 4.71 out of 5 Stars

Ingredients

6 lamb shanks, salt and pepper to taste, 2 table spoons of olive oil, 2 onions, chopped, 3 large carrots, cut into 1/4 inch rounds, 10 cloves of garlic, minced, 1 (750 milliliter) bottle of red wine, 1 (28 ounce) can whole of peeled tomatoes with juice, 1 (10.5 ounce) can of condensed chicken broth, 1 (10.5 ounce) can of beef broth, 5 tea spoons of chopped fresh rosemary, 2 tea spoons of chopped fresh thyme.

Directions

Sprinkle shanks with salt and pepper. Heat oil in heavy large pot or Dutch oven over medium-high heat.

Working in batches, cook shanks until brown on all sides, about 8 minutes. Transfer shanks to plate.

Add onions, carrots and garlic to pot and saute until golden brown, about 10 minutes. Stir in wine, tomatoes, chicken broth and beef broth. Season with rosemary and thyme. Return shanks to pot, pressing down to submerge. Bring to a boil, then reduce heat to medium-low. Cover, and simmer until meat is tender, about 2 hours.

Remove cover from pot. Simmer about 20 minutes longer. Transfer shanks to platter, place in a warm oven. Boil juices in pot until thickened, about 15 minutes. Spoon over shanks.

Nutrition

Per Serving: 481 calories; 21.8 g fat; 17.6 g carbohydrates; 30.3 g protein; 93 mg cholesterol; 759 mg sodium.

Rosemary Braised Lamb Shanks

Ingredients

6 lamb shanks, salt and pepper to taste, 2 table spoons of olive oil, 2 onions chopped, 3 large carrots cut into 1/4 inch rounds, 10 cloves of garlic minced with 1 (750 milliliter) bottle of red wine, 1 (28 ounce) can of whole peeled tomatoes with juice, 1 (10.5 ounce) can of condensed chicken broth, 1 (10.5 ounce) can of beef broth, 5 tea spoons of chopped fresh rosemary, 2 tea spoons of chopped fresh thyme.

Directions

Sprinkle shanks with salt and pepper. Heat oil in heavy large pot or Dutch oven over medium-high heat. Working in batches, cook shanks until brown on all sides, about 8 minutes. Transfer shanks to plate.

Add onions, carrots and garlic to pot and saute until golden brown, about 10 minutes. Stir in wine, tomatoes, chicken broth and beef broth. Season with rosemary and thyme. Return shanks to pot, pressing down to submerge. Bring to a boil, then reduce heat to medium-low. Cover, and simmer until meat is tender, about 2 hours.

Remove cover from pot. Simmer about 20 minutes longer. Transfer shanks to platter, place in a warm oven. Boil juices in pot until thickened, about 15 minutes. Spoon over shanks.

Nutrition Facts

Per Serving: 481 calories; 21.8 g fat; 17.6 g carbohydrates; 30.3 g protein; 93 mg cholesterol; 759 mg sodium.

Texas Ranch Chicken

Rating: 4.16 stars

Ingredients:

2 teaspoons olive oil

1 ½ pounds skinless, boneless chicken parts

1 ½ cups Ranch-style salad dressing

2 cups shredded mozzarella cheese

Directions Checklist

Step 1

Preheat oven to 350 degrees F (175 degrees C). Spread the olive oil in a 9x13 inch baking dish.

Step 2

Arrange chicken in the dish, and cover with the dressing. It's best to place chicken pieces close together so that the cheese and the dressing do not burn on the bottom of the pan.

Step 3

Bake for 20 minutes in the preheated oven. Remove from heat, top with mozzarella cheese, and return to the oven. Continue cooking for about 15 minutes, until the cheese is melted and lightly browned and the chicken is no longer pink and juices run clear.

Nutrition Facts

Per Serving:

543 calories; 45.8 g total fat; 103 mg cholesterol; 863 mg sodium. 3.5 g carbohydrates; 27.6 g protein;

Brown Rice, Broccoli, Cheese and Walnut Surprise

Rating: 4.46 stars

This recipe was born one night when I didn't have too much to do. I guess the only surprise about it is that it tastes so good!

Ingredient Checklist

½ cup of chopped walnuts

1 table spoon of butter

1 onion, chopped

½ tea spoon of minced garlic

1 cup of uncooked instant brown rice

1 cup of vegetable broth

1 pound of fresh broccoli florets

½ tea spoon of salt

⅛ tea spoon of ground black pepper

1 cup of shredded Cheddar cheese

Directions Checklist

Step 1

Preheat oven to 350 degrees F (175 degrees C). Place walnuts on small baking sheet, and bake for 6 to 8 minutes or until toasted.

Step 2

Melt butter in a medium saucepan over medium heat. Cook onion and garlic in melted butter for 3 minutes, stirring frequently. Stir in the rice, add the broth, and bring to a boil. Reduce heat to medium-low. Cover, and simmer until liquid is absorbed, about 7 to 8 minutes.

Step 3

Place broccoli in a microwave-safe casserole dish, and sprinkle with salt and pepper. Cover, and microwave until tender.

Step 4

Spoon rice onto a serving platter, and top with broccoli. Sprinkle walnuts and cheese on top.

Nutrition Facts

Per Serving:

368 calories; 22.9 g total fat; 37 mg cholesterol; 643 mg sodium. 30.4 g carbohydrates; 15.1 g protein;

Indian Style Sheekh Kabab
Rated as 4.62 out of 5 Stars

"This is a spicy and extremely flavorful recipe which will surely be a hit at any BBQ party."

Ingredients

2 pounds of lean ground lamb, 2 onions of finely chopped, 1/2 cup of fresh mint leaves, finely chopped, 1/2 cup of cilantro, finely chopped, 1 table spoon ginger paste, 1 table spoon green chile paste, 2 teaspoons ground cumin, 2 teaspoons ground coriander, 2 teaspoons paprika, 1 teaspoon cayenne pepper, 2 teaspoons salt1/4 cup vegetable oilskewers.

Directions

In a large bowl, mix ground lamb, onions, mint, cilantro, ginger paste, and chile paste. Season with cumin, coriander, paprika, cayenne, and salt. Cover, and refrigerate for 2 hours.

Mold handfuls of the lamb mixture, about 1 cup, to form sausages around skewers. Make sure the meat is spread to an even thickness. Refrigerate until you are ready to grill.

Preheat grill for high heat.

Brush grate liberally with oil, and arrange kabobs on grill. Cook for 10 minutes, or until well done, turning as needed to brown evenly.

Nutrition Facts

Per Serving: 304 calories; 22.6 g fat; 4.7 g carbohydrates; 20.1 g protein; 76 mg cholesterol; 665 mg sodium. Full nutrition

Paleo Pecan-Maple Salmon

Rated as 4.47 out of 5 Stars

"This recipe is not only easy but healthy and tasty! Paleo, gluten-free and dairy-free!"

Ingredients

4 (4 ounce) fillets salmon, salt and ground black pepper to taste, 1/2 cup pecans, 3 table spoons pure maple syrup, 1 table spoon apple cider vinegar, 1 tea spoon smoked paprika, 1/2 teaspoon chipotle pepper powder, 1/2 teaspoon onion powder.

Directions

Place salmon fillets on a baking sheet and season with salt and black pepper.

Combine pecans, maple syrup, vinegar, paprika, chipotle powder, and onion powder in a food processor; pulse until texture is crumbly. Spoon pecan mixture on top of each salmon fillet, coating the entire top surface. Refrigerate coated salmon, uncovered, for 2 to 3 hours.

Preheat oven to 425 degrees F (220 degrees C).

Bake salmon in the preheated oven until fish flakes easily with a fork, 12 to 14 minutes

GLUTEN FREE SIDE DISH

Sugar Snap Peas with Mint
Rated as 4.47 out of 5 Stars

"Simple and quick to prepare. Sugar snap peas are quickly fried with green onion and garlic, and tossed with fresh mint leaves. Wonderful use for spring garden vegetables. Serve hot or at room temperature."

Ingredients

2 tea spoons of olive oil, 3/4 pound sugar snap peas trimmed, 3 green onions chopped, 1 clove garlic chopped, 1/8 teaspoon of salt, 1/8 tea spoon of pepper1 tablespoon chopped fresh mint.

Directions

Heat oil in a large skillet over medium heat. Add the sugar snap peas, green onion, and garlic. Season with salt and pepper. Stir-fry for 4 minutes, then remove from heat and stir in the mint leaves.

Nutrition Facts

Per Serving: 67 calories; 2.4 g fat; 8.3 g carbohydrates; 2.3 g protein; 0 mg cholesterol; 75 mg sodium. Full nutrition

Herbed Mushrooms with White Wine

Rated as 4.53 out of 5 Stars

"Mushrooms are sauteed with your favorite herbs and white wine. Mmm!"

Ingredients

1 tablespoon of olive oil, 1 and 1/2 pounds of fresh mushrooms, 1 tea spoon of Italian seasoning, 1/4 cup dry white wine, 2 cloves of garlic, minced salt and pepper to taste, 2 table spoons chopped fresh chives.

Directions

Heat the oil in a skillet over medium heat. Place mushrooms in the skillet, season with Italian seasoning, and cook 10 minutes, stirring frequently.

Mix the wine and garlic into the skillet, and continue cooking until most of the wine has evaporated. Season with salt and pepper, and sprinkle with chives. Continue cooking 1 minute.

Nutrition Facts

Per Serving: 57 calories; 2.7 g fat; 5.6 g carbohydrates; 2.3 g protein; 0 mg cholesterol; 5 mg sodium. Full nutrition

Fried Plantains

"Fried plantains are a traditional treat in many parts of the world. Try them once and you'll be hooked. Overly ripe plantains work best for this recipe."

Ingredients

1 quart oil for frying and 2 plantains.

Directions

Preheat oil in a large, deep skillet over medium high heat.

Peel the plantains and cut them in half. Slice the halves lengthwise into thin pieces.

Fry the pieces until browned and tender. Drain excess oil on paper towels.

Nutrition Facts

Per Serving: 152 calories; 11.2 g fat; 14.3 g carbohydrates; 0.6 g protein; 0 mg cholesterol; 2 mg sodium

Brandied Candied Sweet Potatoes
Rated as 4.46 out of 5 Stars

Ingredients

2 pounds of sweet potatoes peeled and diced, ½ cup of butter, ½ cup of packed brown sugar, 1/2 cup of brandy, 1/2 teaspoon of salt.

Directions

Place sweet potatoes in a large saucepan with enough water to cover. Bring to a boil. Cook 15 minutes, or until tender but firm. Drain, and set aside.

In a large skillet over low heat, melt the butter. Stir in the brown sugar, brandy, and salt. Add the sweet potatoes, and stir to coat. Cook, stirring gently, until sweet potatoes are heated through and well glazed.

Nutrition Facts

Per Serving: 295 calories; 11.6 g fat; 36.3 g carbohydrates; 1.9 g protein; 31 mg cholesterol; 293 mg sodium.

Corned Beef Potato Pancakes
Rated as 3.82 out of 5 Stars

"This recipe is fantastic for breakfast. Serve with or without eggs. We love these on a Sunday morning."

Ingredients

3 medium potatoes, shredded, 2 green onions, chopped1/2 (12 ounce) can corned beef, broken into very small chunks1 eggsalt and pepper to taste1/4 cup vegetable oilAdd all ingredients to list

Directions

In a large bowl, mix the potatoes, green onions, corned beef, and egg. Season with salt and pepper. Form the mixture into golf ball sized balls.

Heat the oil in a skillet over medium heat. Place the potato balls a few at a time into the skillet, flatten with a spatula, and fry 7 minutes on each side, until crisp and golden brown. Drain on paper towels.

Nutrition Facts

Per Serving: 260 calories; 9 g fat; 28.6 g carbohydrates; 16.3 g protein; 83 mg cholesterol; 451 mg sodium.

Mediterranean Vegetable Cakes
Rated as 4 out of 5 Stars

"I am not a vegan or vegetarian but still really enjoy this recipe. It is similar to one I found on a vegetarian website, however, I made my own additions and now it is amazing! These are an awesome side dish or main dish! They can be served with Parmesan cheese, red or green hot sauce, or olive tapenade, but these are also great by themselves!"

Ingredients

1/4 cup of olive oil divided, 1 cup of finely chopped onions, 3 cloves of garlic chopped, 3 cups of roughly chopped spinach, 1 large parsnip grated, 1/3 cup of chopped artichoke hearts, 1/3 cup of chopped Kalamata olives, 1/3 cup of almond flour, 1/4 cup of finely chopped sun-dried tomatoes, 3 small eggs, beaten, 2 tablespoons finely chopped walnuts, 1/2 a tea spoon salt,1/4 tea spoon of ground black pepper.

Directions

Heat 2 tablespoons olive oil in a skillet over medium heat; cook and stir onion and garlic until onion is softened, about 5 minutes. Add spinach to onion mixture; cook and stir until wilted, about 5 minutes. Transfer onion-spinach mixture to a large bowl and cool slightly, 5 to 10 minutes.

Mix parsnip, artichoke hearts, olives, almond flour, tomatoes, eggs, walnuts, salt, and pepper into onion-spinach mixture; form into 6 cakes.

Heat remaining 2 tablebspoons of olive oil in a skillet. Cook cakes in the hot oil until browned and crispy, about 5 minutes per side.

Nutrition Facts

Per Serving: 223 calories; 15.8 g fat; 15.4 g carbohydrates; 7.1 g protein; 69 mg cholesterol; 446 mg sodium.

"Fonio grains are mixed with aromatic vegetables, sesame seeds, nuts, and raisins for a nutritious alternative to rice pilaf. Serve this with your favorite savory meat or fish dish. Fonio is one of the most forgiving grains out there. It reheats splendidly, too. This dish can be made ahead of time and simply reheated by adding a bit of stock and a turn or two in the microwave."

Ingredients

3/4 cup warm vegetable stock divided, 1/4 cup of golden raisins, 2 table spoons of vegetable oil, 1 shallot minced, 1 clove of garlic minced, 2 tablespoons of black sesame seeds,1/4 cup shredded carrots, 1/3 cup of chopped almonds, 1 cup of fonio grains,1 pinch of salt and freshly ground black pepper to taste, 1/8 cup of pomegranate seeds.

Directions

Combine 1/2 cup of vegetable stock and raisins in a bowl and set aside.

Heat oil in a deep skillet over medium heat. Cook shallot, garlic, black sesame seeds, carrots, and almonds until fragrant and softened, about 4 minutes. Add fonio and stir to absorb flavors, about 2 minutes. Pour in raisins and stock and stir until fonio has absorbed all the liquid, about 5 minutes. Add some remaining stock and cook until the fonio is soft. You may not need the entire amount, depending on the brand and quality of the fonio. Season with salt and pepper.

Remove from heat once all liquid is absorbed. Fluff with a fork and sprinkle with fresh pomegranate seeds before serving.

Nutrition Facts

Per Serving: 789 calories; 28 g fat; 125.4 g carbohydrates; 12.7 g protein; 0 mg cholesterol; 264 mg sodium.

Carrot Cake Quinoa
Rated as 4 out of 5 Stars

"Gluten-free and vegan! A great lunch for work. Healthy and delicious! Serve hot or cold."

Ingredients

4 cups of water, 1 cup of quinoa, 3/4 cup of amaranth, 1/4 cup of wild rice, 2 tea spoons of ground cumin, 1 teaspoon of salt, 2 stalks of celery diced, 1 large carrot grated,1/2 cup of canned chick peas (garbanzo beans) (optional), 1/2 cup of raisins, 1 table spoon of olive oil, 1 clove of garlic minced, salt and ground black pepper to taste.

Directions

Bring water, quinoa, amaranth, wild rice, cumin, and 1 teaspoon salt to a boil in a saucepan. Reduce heat to medium-low, cover, and simmer until grains are tender and water has been absorbed, 20 to 25 minutes. Let stand for 5 minutes.

Mix celery, carrot, chickpeas, raisins, olive oil, garlic, salt, and pepper together in a bowl; add grain mixture and mix well.

Nutrition Facts

Per Serving: 472 calories; 9.2 g fat; 85.1 g carbohydrates; 15.4 g protein; 0 mg cholesterol; 721 mg sodium.

Easy Quinoa Mac And Cheese

"Gluten-free mac & cheese is easy and delicious with quinoa and sharp Cheddar cheese."

2 teaspoons of olive oil, 1 tablespoon of minced onion, 1 clove of garlic, minced, 1 cup of quinoa, rinsed and drained, 2 large eggs, 1 cup non-fat milk, 1 cup of Borden® Sharp Cheddar Shredded Cheese.

Directions

Preheat oven to and spray an 8-inch-square baking dish with non-stick cooking spray.

Heat oil in a medium skillet over medium heat until hot. Add onion and garlic and sauté for 1 minute or until onion is tender. Add quinoa and cook, stirring, until golden brown and toasted, 2 to 3 minutes. Add 2 ½ cups of water, bring to a boil, reduce heat to medium-low and simmer, covered, until water has been absorbed, about 10 minutes. Remove from heat.

Whisk eggs and milk together in a large bowl. Stir quinoa into egg mixture, and whisk in 1/2 cup of the cheese. Spread in the prepared baking dish and sprinkle with remaining 1/2 cup of cheese. Bake for 30 minutes. Garnish with chopped tomato and green onion, if desired. Serve immediately.

Nutrition Facts

Per Serving: 346 calories; 16.5 g fat; 32 g carbohydrates; 18.3 g protein; 124 mg cholesterol; 243 mg sodium.

Cathy's Gluten-Free Oatmeal Waffles
Rated as 4.22 out of 5 Stars

"If you are bored with your morning bowl of oatmeal, here's a great alternative. Make lots of extra, freeze, and toast them on demand. Serve with butter, maple syrup and sliced banana …yummy!"

Ingredients

cooking spray, 1 ½ cup of gluten-free rolled oats, 3/4 cup of almond milk, 1 egg, at room temperature, separated, 3 tablespoons of melted butter, 1 tablespoon of brown sugar, 1 tea spoon of baking powder. Add all ingredients to list

Directions

Preheat a waffle iron according to manufacturer's instructions. Grease with cooking spray.

Combine oats and almond milk in a large bowl.

Whisk egg yolk and butter together in a small bowl; stir into oat mixture.

Beat egg white in a glass, metal, or ceramic bowl until stiff peaks form.

Stir brown sugar and baking powder into the oat mixture. Fold beaten egg white gently into the batter.

Scoop 1/2 cup of batter onto the preheated iron and spread to the edges. Close iron and cook until iron stops steaming, about 5 minutes. Repeat with remaining batter.

Nutrition Facts

Per Serving: 235 calories; 12.4 g fat; 25.9 g carbohydrates; 5.9 g protein; 69 mg cholesterol; 233 mg sodium.

GLUTEN FREE DESSERTS

Buckeyes I
Rating: 4.47 stars

This recipe is so good that I double it whenever I make it. Since it is peanut butter balls dipped in chocolate it is almost like candy. Real buckeyes are nuts that grow on trees and are related to the horse chestnut.

Ingredient Checklist

1 ½ cups of peanut butter

1 cup of butter, softened

½ tea spoon of vanilla extract

6 cups of confectioners' sugar

4 cups of semi sweet chocolate chips

Directions Checklist

Step 1

In a large bowl, mix together the peanut butter, butter, vanilla and confectioners' sugar. The dough will look dry. Roll into 1 inch balls and place on a waxed paper-lined cookie sheet.

Step 2

Press a toothpick into the top of each ball (to be used later as the handle for dipping) and chill in freezer until firm, about 30 minutes.

Step 3

Melt chocolate chips in a double boiler or in a bowl set over a pan of barely simmering water. Stir frequently until smooth.

Step 4

Dip frozen peanut butter balls in chocolate holding onto the toothpick. Leave a small portion of peanut butter showing at the top to make them look like Buckeyes. Put back on the cookie sheet and refrigerate until serving.

Chocolate Chip cookies
Ingredient Checklist

¾ cup of butter, softened

1 ¼ cups of packed brown sugar

¼ cup of white sugar

1 tea spoon of gluten-free vanilla extract

¼ cup of egg substitute

2 ¼ cups of gluten-free baking mix

1 tea spoon of baking soda

1 tea spoon of baking powder

1 tea spoon of salt

12 ounces of semisweet chocolate chips

Directions Checklist

Step 1

Preheat oven to 375 degrees F (190 degrees C). Prepare a greased baking sheet.

Step 2

In a medium bowl, cream butter and sugar. Gradually add replacer eggs and vanilla while mixing. Sift together gluten- free flour mix, baking soda, baking powder, and salt. Stir into the butter mixture until blended. Finally, stir in the chocolate chips.

Step 3

Using a teaspoon, drop cookies 2 inches apart on prepared baking sheet. Bake in preheated oven for 6 to 8 minutes or until light brown. Let cookies cool on baking sheet for 2 minutes before removing to wire racks.

Nutrition Facts

Per Serving:

288 calories; 13.5 g total fat; 20 mg cholesterol; 404 mg sodium. 43.5 g carbohydrates; 2.1 g protein; Full Nutrition

Chocolate Peanut Butter Bars
Ingredients

Ingredient Checklist

½ cup of butter

½ cup of packed brown sugar

1 teaspoon of vanilla extract

2 cups of peanut butter

2 ½ cups of confectioners' sugar

2 cups of semisweet chocolate chips

Directions Checklist

Step 1

Melt butter or margarine over low heat. Add sugars, peanut butter and vanilla. Mix well.

Step 2

Press into a 9 x 13 inch pan.

Step 3

Melt chocolate chips and spread over the top. Cool.

Amazing Gluten-Free Layer Bars

Rating: 4.13 stars

A gluten-free adaptation of the traditional Seven Layer Bar recipe. All ingredients are available in ordinary supermarkets. Be sure to check the packaging on your ingredients to make sure they are indeed gluten-free.

Ingredient Checklist

7 ounces of sweetened flaked coconut, divided

1 cup of butter scotch chips

6 ounces of semisweet chocolate chips

8 ounces of unsalted peanuts

½ cup of sliced almonds

1 (14 ounce) can sweetened condensed milk

Directions Checklist

Step 1

Preheat oven to 350 degrees F (175 degrees C). Generously grease one 13x9-inch baking pan.

Step 2

Spread 2/3 of the flaked coconut evenly on the bottom of the baking pan. Sprinkle the butterscotch morsels, chocolate chips, and peanuts evenly over the coconut layer. Pour condensed milk evenly over the whole pan. Top with sliced almonds and remaining coconut.

Step 3

Bake in preheated oven for 20 minutes. Cool completely before cutting into squares.

Nutrition Facts

Per Serving:

185 calories; 10.9 g total fat; 4 mg cholesterol; 43 mg sodium. 19.7 g carbohydrates; 3.6 g protein;

Perfect Flourless Orange Cake

Rating: 4.33 stars

A beautiful moist light cake with complex and full flavors of oranges and orange peel. Super easy to make, and people love it! Serve in wedges with a mound of whipped cream or ice cream.

Ingredient Checklist

2 whole oranges with peel

6 eggs

1 pinch of saffron powder (optional)

1 ¼ cups of white sugar

½ teaspoon of baking powder

1 ¼ cups of finely ground almonds (almond meal)

1 teaspoon finely chopped candied orange peel (optional)

Directions Checklist

Step 1

Place the oranges in a large saucepan, and add enough water to cover. Bring to a boil, and boil for 2 hours over medium heat. Check occasionally to make sure they do not boil dry. Allow the oranges to cool, then cut them open and remove the seeds. Process in a blender or food processor to a coarse pulp.

Step 2

Preheat the oven to 375 degrees F (190 degrees C). Thoroughly grease a 10-inch round cake pan and line it with parchment paper.

Step 3

In a large bowl, beat the eggs and sugar together using an electric mixer until thick and pale, about 10 minutes. Mix in baking powder and saffron (optional). Stir in the pureed oranges. Gently fold in almond meal and candied orange peel (optional); pour batter into the prepared pan.

Step 4

Bake until a small knife inserted into the center comes out clean, about 1 hour. Allow the cake to cool in the pan. Tap out onto a serving plate when cool.

Nutrition Facts

Per Serving:

174 calories; 8.6 g total fat; 70 mg cholesterol; 42 mg sodium. 21 g carbohydrates; 5.4 g protein;

Lemon Souffle
Rated as 3.71 out of 5 Stars

1 egg, 1 large lemon, zested and juiced, 1/4 cup of castor sugar or super fine sugar, 1 tea spoon of corn starch, 2 table spoons of unsalted butter, cubed 3 egg whites, 5 table spoons of castor sugar or super fine sugar, 3 egg yolks, 1 large lemon, zested and juiced, 2 table spoons of confectioners' sugar for dusting.

Directions

Preheat the oven to 350 degrees F (175 degrees C).

Whisk the egg in a medium saucepan, and mix in the 1 lemon's zest and juice, 1/4 cup sugar and cornstarch. Set over medium heat, and cook stirring constantly until the mixture thickens. Reduce heat to low, and continue whisking for another minute. Remove from the heat and stir in the butter. Divide between four 6 or 8 ounce ramekins. Set aside.

In a medium glass or metal bowl, whip egg whites with an electric mixer. When they are able to hold a soft peak, sprinkle in 1 table spoon of the sugar, and continue mixing until stiff. Whisk the remaining 4 table spoons of sugar into the egg yolks along with the zest and juice of the remaining lemon. Fold a couple of spoonfuls of the egg whites into the yolks to lighten them up, then fold in the rest of the whites. Spoon into the ramekins over the lemon curd, and run a finger around the inside of each rim.

Place the ramekins onto a baking sheet, and place in the preheated oven. Bake for 15 to 17 minutes, until puffed and golden brown. Let cool for about 5 minutes before serving.

Nutrition Facts

Per Serving: 256 calories; 10.5 g fat; 38.9 g carbohydrates; 7 g protein; 215 mg cholesterol; 68 mg sodium.

Irish Potato Candy

Rating: 4.36 stars

A cute little confection that looks just like little potatoes. This kind does not contain potatoes; they are made using cream cheese and coconut.

Ingredient Checklist

¼ cup of butter, softened

½ (8 ounce) package cream cheese

1 tea spoon of vanilla extract

4 cups of confectioners' sugar

2 ½ cups of flaked coconut

1 table spoon of ground cinnamon

Directions Checklist

Step 1

In a medium bowl, beat the butter and cream cheese together until smooth. Add the vanilla and confectioners' sugar; beat until smooth. Using your hands if necessary, mix in the coconut. Roll into balls or potato shapes, and roll in the cinnamon. Place onto a cookie sheet and chill to set. If desired, roll potatoes in cinnamon again for darker color.

Nutrition Facts

Per Serving:

59 calories; 2.3 g total fat; 4 mg cholesterol; 20 mg sodium. 9.7 g carbohydrates; 0.3 g protein;

Angel Food Candy
Rated as 4.53 out of 5 Stars

Sugar and dark corn syrup are cooked with vinegar and tempered with baking soda to make a crunchy candy that gets covered in a chocolate coating."

Ingredients:

1 cup of white sugar, 1 cup of dark corn syrup, 1 table spoon of vinegar, 1 table spoon baking soda, 1 pound of chocolate confectioners' coating.

Directions

Butter a 9x13 inch baking dish.

In a medium saucepan over medium heat, combine sugar, corn syrup and vinegar. Cook, stirring, until sugar dissolves. Heat, without stirring, to 300 to 310 degrees F (149 to 154 degrees C), or until a small amount of syrup dropped into cold water forms hard, brittle threads.

Remove from heat and stir in baking soda. Pour into prepared pan; do not spread. (Mixture will not fill pan.) Allow to cool completely.

In the microwave or over a double boiler, melt coating chocolate, stirring frequently until smooth. Break cooled candy into bite-sized pieces and dip into melted candy coating. Let set on waxed paper. Store tightly covered.

Nutrition Facts

Per Serving: 129 calories; 6 g fat; 22.2 g carbohydrates; 1.2 g protein; 0 mg cholesterol; 135 mg sodium

Conclusion

Gastroparesis is either temporary or chronic. It can be a symptom of another condition, or it can be idiopathic, which means the cause is unknown.

No matter what the cause or duration of your gastroparesis, eating small meals and limiting your fiber and fat intake can help your digestion.

Different people with different diagnoses can tolerate certain food items better than others. Always speak with your doctor about your individualized nutritional needs while treating gastroparesis.

It's important to make sure that your body is still getting the vitamins and minerals necessary for healthy organ function as you recover from your gastroparesis symptoms.

Changing what and how you eat can help you to stay energized and healthy when you have gastroparesis. But it will probably take a bit of trial and error to find what works best for you. Unfortunately, there is no single gastroparesis diet that relieves symptoms for everyone. Stay connected to your healthcare team as you journey through the experience of experimenting with foods and meal timing.

CPSIA information can be obtained
at www.ICGtesting.com
Printed in the USA
LVHW040158240223
740335LV00015B/835